# AT THE END OF THIS SUMMER

# JOHN HAINES

## *At the End of This Summer*

POEMS, 1948–1954

COPPER CANYON PRESS

Publication of this book is supported by a grant from the National Endow-
ment for the Arts and a grant from the Lannan Foundation. Additional sup-
port to Copper Canyon Press has been provided by the Andrew W. Mellon
Foundation, the Lila Wallace–Reader's Digest Fund, and the Washington
State Arts Commission. Copper Canyon Press is in residence with Centrum
at Fort Worden State Park.

Author photo by Peggy Davis.

*Library of Congress Cataloging-in-Publication Data*
Haines, John Meade, 1924–
At the end of this summer: poems, 1948–1954 / by John Haines.
p. cm.
ISBN 1-55659-079-2 (pbk.)
I. Title.
PS3558.A33A93 1997
811'.54 – dc21    97-21180

COPPER CANYON PRESS
P.O. BOX 271, PORT TOWNSEND, WASHINGTON 98368

## ACKNOWLEDGMENTS

The author wishes to thank the editors of the following magazines in which some of these poems were first published: *Willow Springs, Third Coast, Red Mud Review, Sparrow, Black Moon, The Hudson Review, Pemmican, ELF, Gale, Measure.*

# CONTENTS

## III. *New York, 1951–52*

## IV. *California, 1952–54*

The poems in this volume represent an early period of apprenticeship, most of them written while I was a student in Washington, D.C. and New York City during the late 1940s and early 1950s. The poems were crowded into a time when I was still very much involved in my art studies, but also reading intensely in both verse and prose, exploring the potential in my growing commitment to poetry.

This present gathering is a selection from the many poems I wrote at that time in one form or another – lyrics, narratives, meditative sequences and dramatic episodes – while under the influence of one admired poet or another. It would not be too much to say that at some point in that early period I had simply caught fire with the written word, a passion that held me in spite of every obstacle and momentary distraction.

This book is divided into four sections, each devoted to the time and place in which the poems were written. As I reread them now, the poems revive in me moments of fleeting perception in Washington and New York, as well as in Provincetown and, later, in California. I wrote then with little sense of revision, all the while searching for my own voice, living by one means or another, and looking forward to an eventual return to my home place in Alaska. It was an intense and fruitful time, much of it shared with my first wife and fellow student of art, Peggy Davis.

For the most part, and despite an occasional note of approval, the poems found no acceptance among the editors to whose journals I sometimes sent a small group. The one bracing encouragement came early in 1953, in a letter from William Carlos Williams, to whom I had sent a few of my poems, seeking an opinion. His reply, generous and honest, restored a good deal of my sometimes faltering confidence. At the center of his remarks was a warning that I should not expect quick success. As things turned out, it was a prophetic insight.

I am particularly grateful to Sam Hamill and Copper Canyon Press, that these poems, written so many years ago, may at last find a readership.

John Haines
December 1996

*For Peggy Elizabeth Davis*

# AT THE END OF THIS SUMMER

Storm over Tenderfoot,
rain on the Dome.
Our berry cans are full,
it's time to go home.

# 1. *Washington–New York, 1948–50*

# Departure

The road darkens toward the west,
toward the town,
the sky blown clear of all but the fringes
of lemon light;
still the air will shape to the sight
remembered forms.

The turning leaf falls on the ground
that felt the foot,
the waters murmur of the river
that turns away,
the flood of night harms no sound
of the birds that are going down
on the unseen horizon.

And darker, the final bearing
toward the wings
that wait in gathered cloth for one
who needs no eyes
to see the drifting heartbreak
of the smoky hills.

## November You

Why is it and how, wherever I go,
your face before me, now that the trees
are all naked and white,
and the leaves lie on the ground, unburied.

Why do I witness your hair
in the withered grass? How is it I see
your forehead among the mass
of somber hills, brown with hunger,
and why am I facing
your breath in Decembering winds,

now that the sky is aged and wrinkled,
with the air fleshed to the bone?

Why are the trees so suddenly alone,
as I am home yet homeless,
and hear the sound of your voice
walking the floor?

Why do your footsteps approach
but never come by the watching door,
as your eyes appear in the darkness,
to glimmer and sink away
behind the mirror where I look –

now that the sun is gone
and the world is gray with November,
as the fires of this room, unfed by you,
are dead, and I remember:

on blackening panes a numbing rain
shot through with fear.

Are they your tears falling silently
upon the winding-sheet of November?
And am I here, wintering by
your absent feet, one separate ember?

Why is it the night comes on
so swiftly? I am so cold.

# I am a Tree, Very Quiet are My Leaves

I am a tree, very quiet are my leaves
On a still day,
And in summer, many.
Urged on by wind, my leaves sometimes
Become wild and shout among themselves;
Other times they merely whisper.
But always in autumn they fall,
Turning over, many-colored, their frail
Bodies to the sun.
I gave up long ago trying to catch them.

I have grown old standing here –
I who have watched my withered leaves
Gathering at my feet
And the gloomy masses piling overhead;
Who have felt the tiny pulse of early April,
Heard the great voice of the summer sky:
I have grown old,
But I still stand,
I still feel, in winter, my strong roots
Beneath the snow.

Some speak of the end of the world,
But I know:
Come summer, then autumn,
Come winter and spring,

I shall never stop growing.

# Song

I shall live in the candlelight of your eyes,
Desiring no more of the sun,
Dreaming no dreams,
Lying down with a sigh,
And of death: only that sleep
Which is sweet and cannot die
The more.
            With the peace
Of ten thousand years shall there disclose
None but the drying of tears
And the gleaming. Take these hands,
Their touch shall be
The cleansing of pain and the feeling,
But the believing is to be found
Wrapped in a sheet of grass.

By your fingers I am born
To wait and, by removal, stretch my own;

I say, though my grave is empty.

# Magic

Like a walk in the jungle of that dark country,
Forever your creeping hair;
As a day-drink in that green-hinged night thirst,
Always the floating of your eyes
Binds me and my outer wish
In the serious dream
Of folded roots.

Like magic, he said, it is only the hanging moon
And the black whisper of water,
And the swaying of moss in no wind
Like a spell.

Something of the sea dragging at the dumbness
Of rocks long away on the end
Of the soul's refuge:

What have you to say?
Are you only water    water
Salt and sea water?

Again, the river where your hands run like
The soft nuzzle of flesh,
Darkness where your lips close on the dead song
With no sound but the stealthy rain padding,
And the path is a prisoner as myself
With the green dampness closing,
The jungle drinking:

Like magic, he said, it is only the bleeding fern
And the stars falling out of their sockets,
And the cypress standing on no ground
Like a spell.

# Poem for a Drowned Child

Beyond these
    Fairy fields and the still flashing through fog
Of wet morning wings
And the call in sea grass
    Of the close-hauling land;

Beyond this,
    Tall winds, and a warning among trees
Cries in the looking nest
Of gull and cormorant
    And the white home of mist.

Beyond these
    High tides and the wild wish of water-rocks
Combing the wave
And the search in drubbed sand
    For an answering shell;

Beyond this,
    The lull and question in the trades shift
The lost legends of a dead
Child to the listening
    Chambers of the drowned.

## Poem

Not for this time nor that alone
Shall I forget your face, dear girl –
Moon of the last rising,
Nor that single part of dark which forms
My life; not for these
Nor the fragment intervals

That crown the years, but for the night
That shall eternal hide this martyred light.

And where you sleep, may I always
Stand, as that breath of love
And promised waking stands:
The hand hovering and almost descending
To your cheek where may
Those terrors never touch as known

By others. And not for poems should you weep,
But for the other arms that lie asleep.

# Night Falls Once

Sometimes I think the night is like a wandering
Shroud, looking for a head to wear it;
Like the ghost of old religions come back
To haunt the grown-up child where he walks alone
In ways he walks but once. So, I think,
For what could be the moving theme in that pulling
Of blinds, and behind them the turned-off light
And, after that, the eyelids drawn across
The brain, but that a man is somewhere winding
A sheet about his head and crossing his breast
With a dream that says, God.
                     And in the city,
As if for a last time, the winking off
Of nightclub signs, the man who locks his door,
Who sheds brutality from his shoulders and wipes
The madness from his face; the smoke drifting
Away from the dark, reluctant stacks, the stray
Cat that crouches in its shy corner,
And that single one who would be hurrying
Somewhere from one streetlamp to another: these
Know the fatal garment and the damp hands
That adjust the wearer.
                  As though that dawn we witnessed
Once in the singing time had gone astray
In those fields and, searching, gathered all
The light in its arms and wandered away, down
The dim country of the unborn.

And not my hand or eye alone shall this night
Close; do you not hold the image
Off with a clenched smile? Do you not hide
Your face in someone's hair and whisper that
The time is short? And may you feel the shadow

Hover and the breath go stale, the arms
You know recede, and your lips left clinging
To the darkness of your canceled sight:
Night falls but that once, though
A million dawns were stacked against the brain.

## To Remember Another Time

Helen, beyond all accustomed beauty I place you,
Shining alone. In a dead king's dream
Of conquest and vengeance, in a wrong-headed youth's
    desire, another's
     Dream dissolved in loss –
In these you figured, and the possibility of how
    many others.

And if we think of strong women with bloody hands,
Hate in their hearts, and about them crashing
Pillars and dust raining from the mouths of murdered
    sons
     And daughters: you are more
Than myth; in the shadow of your quiet stature these
    things pale.

Well, at peace, you for whom two cities warred.
The fallen crowns gather mould,
The walls and towers lie fire-blackened stones, the
    thieves and avengers
     Are separate with their dreams,
And you still bright, the remaining star in a darkened
    land.

## A Dream of Love

That day we bridged the inevitable gulf.
The river ran south
and we walked north beside it;
and that was morning,
feeling to us somewhat of early spring
though we stood deep in October
with the handfuls of leaves and flowers
in a bird-departed country.
It was a day in which to forget.
Did you forget,
     that day,
the others living perhaps somewhere
as if they could take this from you?
I forgot many things,
watching you step across
the shallows and bend to pick a stone,
and where I waded the water
was cold enough and the sand soft
to revive only pleasure.

So we left the river, still hearing it
through the trees and faded shrubs,
taking a path into the woods
where the hill mounted and would lead down
again. I knew the way
that would bring us beneath the falls,
but I let you travel first, and I
could watch you climbing the rocks
and fallen trees, the old earth-gathered
timbers yet like fences
although forgotten, looking back sometimes
at me to smile. I saw
the falls before they were visible

through the web of limbs, as I knew them
rushing toward the final plunge in faltering
leaps until committed
on the ending boulders in froth and thunder;
and when we came beneath them
and stood in the spray
it was just like that and beautiful,
though now I seem to remember mostly the sunlight
glinting on your dark hair.

And it was noon.
There under the deep-falling water
the sun invited us to shed our clothing,
but we waited.
I knew many things about you,
even through the unspoken levels of silence
that lay between us, for our silence
seemed taken up in the water's roaring
and filled with all our thoughts.
        I have almost forgotten how it felt to lie
in such perfect warmth, alive,
undesirous of movement, suspended
over eternity by so slender a thread.

And afterwhile we climbed
to a slope above the falls. Its gentleness
came to us through the cool, sweet grass
still shaded by the remaining leaves
of those more reluctant trees.
And there in the warm and murmurous solitude
we sat and slowly ate, still guarded
by our own comprehending silence.

As if there was more I wanted to know of you,
though now it seems beyond
my memory, more than had come to me

across our peace, I broke it at last.
Our words began the imagination
of spring and became a ghost of summer
in the joy of whispering
our names and fortunes as belonging
to each other. And soon
we were playing, rolling about on the grass
with flung leaves, and dried twigs
for gentle switches, putting off,
            one by one,
our autumn garments
in the flush of that believable summer.
The slope echoed with our shouts
and laughter as I think it still must bear
the imprint of our bodies.
        For a time I became a child again,
and there I was not alone,
for by your voice and innocent freedom
I knew you also had found the way.
We brought with us into that golden siding
a delicate tenderness that was new,
there and to us.
                The peace returned
in the somnolence of afternoon,
and therein we lay and drifted on the streams
of sunlight shored with the passing shadows
under the great flowing sky,
barely awake and listening in the stillness.

And so evening surprised us,
and with a scarcely perceptible chill
bidding us rise and gather after
our scattered things, and follow
down the path we had taken
among the dried and nodding stems
of floral harvest…

Now darkening,
the trees around us merging into gloom
and seasonal faith we could not deny.
    You surely remember –
didn't we walk beside the river again,
now in its one direction
we followed through the descending darkness,
and by its murmur
toward the single road that led
out of the summer's memory and ours,
into the frost of another and more mindful time,
and not together – no, alone.

# Song

As if my love were like the bending year:
Bleak marvel I look upon with tenderness,
There is no outcast singing, she rides high
In a maze of cloudy passion, a tower of seeming,
Drunk with the snowless winds
That cry for that white veiling. Oh, more than present,
Long ago we felt the parched leaves fall –
Be gathered with them, you mindless snore of death.
Desire is mine; it is like that hopeful turning
When the earth sleeps beneath a blanket of sorry
Dead and does not move, appears unwatchful,
And yet, fair girl, she dreams.

## II. Provincetown, 1950–51

## At the End of This Summer

I wonder if I frightened you,
Coming as I did from behind
As you sat alone in your chair
With the low sun melting over your head.
I couldn't imagine what you were
Looking at or thinking of –
You who have always been so lively
And little given to quiet –
And the desire to bend and kiss your hair
Was almost unbearable.
                      You turned,
With that air of half-astonishment
You use so well, I smiled a greeting.

After that, we sat and talked for a while
And enjoyed the departing light.
Then the warmth was gone,
And we rose, I to take my leave, and you
To close the door and pull the shade,
And turn to the lighting of a lamp,
The starting of a fire in the stove.

## Reluctant Music

That time now and what I feel of compelling essence:
By day the wind has been rising,
And now with early darkness the rain comes.
The way I have been walking,
And the streets I have passed, these are deserted;
The houses locked and shuttered against the storm,
And the season is over. The trees bend
And toss in the wind, the wires overhead
Moan as they stretch, and there are
Leaves descending quickly
To lie in gathering pools of water.

A piano sounds from an empty house.
A detached thing, it startles one,
Breaking upon the atmosphere; you wonder
About the hands that are passing
Over the keys, and if they are very much alive.
And as you go on up the street,
It does not follow you;
You almost doubt that you heard it,
The tune not worth recalling,
Just the sound echoing in the memory.

Now this door I unlock and open, step
Through and close behind me,
Exposing myself to the chilly breath of a room
Where I shall light a single lamp,
Draw down the shades,
And without removing any clothing
Pull a chair up to a table,
And sit for a long while, running my hands over a book.

# Admission

Know it then, my girl,
There's little common ground for us.
It was an hour ago or less,
We sat in the sun's warmth
And talked and breathed each other's
Breath, and for that briefness I loved you.
But over the hedge your hair formed
I was amazed and disconcerted
To see my thoughts travel out into
The yard where some men were
Collecting the garbage, there
To stand in question at their activity.
And the words you were whispering
In my ear suddenly became very much
Involved with the rake one of
The men was employing. When
I sought to regain the idea of you and me,
I was confused and felt myself
Lost somewhere behind your back.

\*

We really can't expect to have everything.
You have your own ideas and opinions,
And as vague or incomprehensible
As they may seem to me, they suit you.
I may desire to change some of them,
And I may even try a little, but I don't
Intend to break my back over it.
    And I have mine.
They are surely my own, and excepting
Some heavenly revelation, it is
Extremely doubtful that they will be

Changed or altered, save as they were
Formed, by experience and a ripening
Of conclusion.
                    The clothes you wear
Are not as I would have them –
They remind me a little too much
Of my mother. You douse your face with
Creams before retiring – that too is
Distasteful and strikes a note in memory.
The way you hold a cup and smoke
A cigarette is too calculated toward
Appearances, and you are careful to say
Only the obvious, noncommittal,
And inoffensive things. Your desires
Concerning my rooms and clothing are not
To my liking – you would have curtains
And rugs and flowers and other comforts,
And I should be dressed more neatly
And have my hair cut. But the bare
Walls and rough furnishings are nearer
To me, and a floor littered with
Cigarette butts and scraps of paper is not
Against my will; also, my greasy
Trousers and unironed shirts suit me
More, as does my ragged head.

On the other hand, I have no doubt
That my views as to the inadvisability
Of marriage – more, my dislike of all
Such institutions, and my lack of conviction
That children are a worthy thing – these
And the many other faults, if such they
Be, do little to comfort
Or assure you, and even offend.

But for all this, we may have
Our moments. We can sit in the sun
And be warm, you can have
Your head resting against my raised
Knee and your arms around my
Waist, and your eyes closed; and I will
Remember to bend my head over and kiss
Your nose and cheeks and lips,
And move my hands over your shoulders
And neck. I will not forget to
Murmur something now and then into your
Dreaming ear, and I will try
Just as long and hard as I can to ignore
The busy singing of crickets in the grass outside.

## Even With Your Going and Almost the Sorrow

Even with your going and almost the sorrow
I am content. I retain such things
As you have given me:
A moment in time which was rest,
A further understanding of what it means
To be alone. I would not have sat down, thus
To call my heart to account,
It is not to be blamed. I must look farther
Into darkness to fix the habit
Born of blindness and the child's disease.

Because I have been human and sometimes erred
In thinking myself more than I was,
Although in the clarity of reason I might
Have seen the plain divergence
And recognized the proper path; this,
Because I knew it was not meant
That I should walk without stumbling,
Or because I thought that nothing is
But in relation to its opposite,
I went for a while in the wrong direction.

I guess I wanted to lose myself, to forget
That I had somewhere to go, something
To do. But it was without the climate
Of conviction, and by that lack I turned
And sought my old way.
                              You may go on,
Believing you have left nothing
Of importance behind you, and I will have time
To think and something else to nurture.

# On a Point of Departure

I had thought it would be different
After their various goings:
There would be the time I had been waiting for,
When all their faces melted in one
Last glow of the summer,
And in the after-cooling of light
This small world belonging to me.
And what I wanted, time
To sleep and awaken, to investigate my thoughts
And make of them what I could,
Also appearing and belonging.

There was only you and I among the ruins.
Of all those faces, yours alone remained,
As I had wished. We walked
The streets that had fallen asleep,
Wandered on the moors and beaches
Without company except the birds, and in
Those days that were the warmest
Sought the waters of the bay,
Touched by a sun that was the kinder
For its fading. I thought
You were beautiful, and I said so,
Feeling in your contact that perfect knowledge
Which is love. And what I wrote
Was for you because of what you gave me
And you took nothing away.

It was like a basin of clear water,
Cool and sparkling freshness, in which you might see
All there was and know it yours.
But I smiled in this reflection
Without knowing my heart's content.

I didn't think there might be in myself
That winter spoilage, and therein
Lay the sad surprise. For as we sat
In the dying garden, children
Came to us, laughing, and gathered about
Your knee; and I hated them because
They seemed to love you. It was
What I could not hide, and I know
You saw, for you turned and looked at me,
And in your eyes I read
The time and what it meant.
                                    You went down
From the garden alone. I remained,
Standing amid the faded shrubbery with
The children who looked at me
And were afraid, and then they crept away.

# Picture for a Breakfast Room

Lean upon the table, rest
your head in your hand
    and stare at the early patterns
that mottle the finished plate,
the empty coffee cup.
    Let the warm light you see
before you, molting dust,
mean that which lays and tangles
    in your hair
and which you do not see.

And let another watch you from
across the table through
    a hazy fragrance, who is
also motionless and
struck with the balance of the hour:
    the tranquil burning
of a cigarette, the light fallen
    upon the floor,
the humming warmth outside:
    morning for a day.

## September Song

Sweetened with rain, how often will
this place be sought,
        and with what strange impatience
after a dry summer.
Or when the tide creeps in through
the rushes and weeds, and
        that water spills over into
quiet music:
the curlews and pipers are distant
with seasonal cries, and for
        your sake only the wind motions
the tiny plum leaves
and whispers,
                        Come away, come away.

# The Way West

Maybe there'll come a time again
when the dawn will find
    us ready – the breakfast fires burned out
and banked with sand, their
remnant smoke curling up unstirred
by any wind; and the chill,
    still dewy air will find us ready, the heavy
gear stowed and lashed,
the patched tents struck, the stock
roped in and hitched...
    And one voice calls from a full belly, and
one hand ahead is lifted
and motioned forward – then shoulders
to yoke, buttocks to leather,
    wood squeaking on wood, the wheels beginning
to roll, cries on the warming
air. And the way is down into
the valley, with grass,
    to dust and running water, to buffalo dung
and the far hills,
before the sun drinks west.

# Windsong

How about the wind,
    what does that mean?

Over the long, sharp grass
each grain
of sand and every pebble on
    the long shore
hearing a different sound that is the same.

Fair day, cold day, blow
    and wonder what it's good for.

Sometimes it gets all mixed
up with the sea-
wash, and there's no telling;
    but then it's free
and the morning-wet gulls scream over it...high

But then again blow, and
    what kind of song is that?

Here in a land-forgotten house,
hearing it too,
not quite the same but still
    no different,
watching the beach grass bend and shake its head –

How about the wind,
    what *does* that mean?

# Nocturnal

Missing the noise of the sea at night,
I find it difficult to sleep.
    Difficult to be content with the tame
sounds of human habitation:
somebody's dog barking, somebody's
door swinging to,
a window raised in a nearby house,
the hum and crunch of a passing car...
    And not long for the primitive rhythm
of the tides, the peep of the pewits,
and the sound of the wind in the grass.

# Pictures and Parables

I

Beginning with autumn in another
country, I took one way
of traveling.
    The road led down among
the trees, its ground,
untrodden, was firm and spangled
with the fallen leaves.
    I heard the chickadees
near at hand, and
the far-off signals of south-
flying geese; the river below the hill
was gentle in its bed,
    with voices murmuring, telling
the dying days for my departure.
    The air of that time was chill
in substance, glittering at a distance.

II

I stopped to look at the bird –
the bird moved on.
    It seemed to have a broken leg,
And went hop  hop  hop
across the sand on the other.
    It didn't try to fly,
and I don't think it was afraid;
but every time I approached the bird
the bird moved on.

III

There was an aging man who went
to live in a cave.
   He cast off clothing and hid
his nakedness with rags.
   He bound himself to the rock
with chains and fasted, sustained
only by the gifts of a few who were
   attracted to his state.
He suffered and prayed for the sins of men,
and his name spread about
   the country and grew in fame
with the excellence of his deeds.
   Passing by the cave these latter days,
we see the chains hanging loose
and rusty, and the emptiness of the cave
   is very evident,
for now he has a mountain all to himself
above a worshiping city.

IV

Let us believe in a strong god,
   who makes the oceans
roar and the wind crack about our ears;
who pushes mountains down
upon our cities and parts the seeming
   solid earth to engulf us.
For we are envious of this, and to
believe in a gentle god,
   therefore, does not become us.

V

Late locust
    singing in the long grass,
and the earth is one.
    How shall we faultless dead sing
when the year is gone?


VI

The city of God is very old
and has seldom been entered,
much less settled in.
    The city of men, on the other hand,
is comparatively new
and from the very start has had abundant
commerce and countless settlers.
    Standing on the highway now
where the roads diverge –
one empty, not so cared for, leading
to the ancient of God,
the other paved and thronged with
    accompanying crowds –
which way do you go? I long for
    room and quiet.


VII

This is the sea, and I
have come to know a great
deal about it, noting
its moods, counting the tides, listening
    to the many voices
that are at last but one voice.

And yet sometimes
I think I understand very little
about it, and that is
the fascination of the sea.

VIII

In the evening, and just before
the first stars appear,
the wind rises,
        to blow and make its music
in the slender grass
and about the loose ends of the house,
all night long.
        And you will be
surprised to see how the wind abates
before the last stars dim
into the coming dawn.

IX

Leaving a valley, preparing to go
to the mountains or to the seashore,
you pause and look carefully
about you for anything you may have
left that would be of use to you
in the new climate.
        Leaving the house of the dead
to go out into the sunlight
of the living, you quickly glance about
you and discover there is
No! nothing that you desire or
could ever use again.

X

Time has laid a father's hand
    on my shoulder
and pointed out a long, dark road,
saying: That is your way,
this is not your country, but
    one of travel and
another's home. Yours is there, beyond,
    nor is there other.

# None Coming After

None coming after
will find his steps leading
as these into the stony
garden, missing the musical sound
of water and the rustle of dry
leaves drawn over
the pebbles; a man grown old,
finding his way among
the dwarfish pines whose shallow roots
he trod in passing.
    The sand once holding the
print of his shoe
projected in the long falling light,
shifted and blown.

             None coming after
will tear a leaf from this bush
or stoop beneath these
trees to feel the lower branches
brush across his forehead,
reminded of another
who passed before that autumn
ended, how long ago.

             None coming after
will penetrate the miniatures
of a faded landscape, silent of crickets,
empty of memory,
seeking a place where the water
and leaves still hide,
reminded of one who had gone before,
whom none will follow.

III. *New York, 1951–52*

# In the Museum of Natural History

They stand on a hillside, feeding.
He raises and tosses his head, the nostrils
widen and he blows through them;
but there is no danger. She continues
to feed. Clumps of long, yellow
grass, a few rough gray boulders
sunk in the dry soil that shows between
the grasses; another feeds quietly
a little beyond these two. Down
the long slope, at the bottom, against
the flank of the opposite hill, the river
bends and widens where a patch
of willows gathers over the deepening
pool; you can almost hear
the river, murmuring and whispering
against the banks and farther down
where it shallows on the many stones.
        A lone bird sails over
the dark water of the pool, its wings
glancing in the descending chill and dew.
Above and behind them all, the sky
flares over the mountainous horizon
for the sun's disappearance,
though in that part of the sky most
nearly overhead a few white
clouds stand against the evening.

## Totem

How dark you are, you wooden image –
whose vanished world do you contain?
    Your great, hooked beak
that is only one of your several faces,
over what glacial inlet pointed its
    smiling power?
And under what majesty of fir and spruce
did you stand, outfacing them,
where a race of brown men passed in fear
    and recognition of your silence?
Those were loving and respectful hands
that carved your deep-eyed force –
    the hands of children
working in quiet wood, aware of life's essential
cruelty. A lordly thing you seem
because of that, of a time when violence was –
    what? A consecration.
It is as though you breathed and stones
could speak, telling their dark secrets;
    and water screamed
of blood and tumbling entrails, fallen heads
and members – and you smiled over it all,
    that my hands might touch
the centuries. These halls are too small
for you; an edifice of my time will not contain
you and your world in its mockery.
You were better on that primal shore, and we
    in a dim cellar.

# Interview

My people:
    I am no specialist in matter,
organic or otherwise;
I have studied a little, found some
comfort in looking at
pictures and reading over old
collections,
    smiling at the finned and spike-
toothed oddities that groped
in the slime, feeling something of
terror at a glimpse
of the club-footed monsters that once
roamed uncontradicted
    over this globe – horned automatons,
not measuring their
racial allotments – in that perhaps
more fortunate.
And yet, considering the balance
of things,
    it is a marvel to me at times
how much you have built
and devoured, destroyed and replaced,
against the mills
that move and grind anyway,
and I must look
    with amazement on your separate
faces, not finding that
special sign that might explain it all.
How old are you,
friend? A half-inch of bright wire
on a two-
    billion-mile spool? I think of
geological indications

and wonder, as the age retreats, what
moraines will your head-
bones form at the terminals of Time?

# Similitude

I think of a man flaying the earth
with a long whip: his teeth
are gritted, his muscles strain, and sweat
pours from his brow as time and time
again he lifts the long, black
snake of leather over his steaming
shoulder and brings it down hard
on the bare, dusty ground
with an ear-splitting smack.

And I know what it is to go
into the woods in early spring
with a heavy axe, choose a slender birch,
and carefully balanced on
my feet in the melting snow, swing
and feel the sharp edge biting
into the soft, wet flesh of the tree.

# I Will Tell You How It Was in My Country

In those days

forming that known world
                    of much sun
and little rain,
the broadest of valleys, and a river,
at once contained and containing.

   Where the river flowed
the ground was fertile,
crops were grown, and trees,
and among the trees
were wells
            and people bathing.

   Native stone
raised a city,
the city housed a swarm
      who were
particular of trade and office,

and the gods had temples
                    raised to their diligence.

The sweat of myriads changed
the horizon,
            dynasties were built upon it,
and evidence of wealth
and nobility was seen among many.

So indulged, the divinities
were kind, and for a thousand years
no conqueror appeared.

                    There
was born, and lived,
prospered, declined and died,
    a man,
honorably buried,
                    very long ago.

# From Adjacent Fields

From adjacent fields,
and even a common soil
(perhaps sown and tended by
a common hand)
     – that some migrant germ
should lodge in one,
or that some contour in the other
should favor more the sun,
or that the water in the ground
should run there
better than in the first –
     that one field fully
flowers and lasts throughout
     the summer,
while the seeds of the other
rot in the ground
or, rising a little, wither
before the harvest.

# And Now

Upon the frost
and the sumac smoke,
on the fired stains of the leaves
and in the ashy limbs,
    once more
the unsolicited summer blows back:
whispers of feet
and rainy fingers,
the caravan of trembling voices
sounds through the corridored earth
    brave songs.
Yet shall the music awaken old gods?
Who calls you from among the faded stems –
    laughter,
bright water, quivering
rushes and sunlit stones –
who knows where
they've gone and how?
Green seasons past, you cannot answer.
    Come away,
journeyer – now look down,
the dark untraveled
road, before
you say farewell.

# The Riders

This is the forest – Marta, are you there?
I see the lights,
    this is the place – Marta, Marta!
The lights of that place dimming
from the windows, yellow, a dim golden falling.
    Look, Marta, how that light
spreads and falls upon the frosty ground!

    Ah, it is pale October!
The moonlight spans the clearing and soaks
the forest – the stones
are white and hard by the shrunken stream,
    the forest is still.

We remember – remember the terror that stole
through the wood
    when the riders came nudging their horses
along the gleaming streambed...

    Ah, Marta, remember!
This is the place, the ground is shivered
with ghosts, and the echoes
of their hoofs falling among the frosty stones
    by the dwindled stream.

And the shadows of those and their horses –
we saw them filing in silence
among the trees, only the hoofs of their horses
    clicking upon the pebbles –
half seen, half known to us, filing between
    the thick black trunks
under the silvered needle-clusters, the click
and start of metal on frozen stone...

Toward that light spilling through rustic glass
to yellow the gloom
    where the logwall hid the moon
and the frost hung out its keys.


    And the night drew close:
the hoofs were stopped, the clearing swam
in a glittering pool of silence
with the sharp, dark forms of riders and horses
        clustering out
where the house was a blotch in the silver,
the gold of its windows gone.


    We were away in the night,
but we heard behind us the plundered door,
the screech of the boards,
    the burst and sprinkle of glass
fallen in frozen weeds...
    And then the split of that scream,
the naked soul cut off,
    and the ghost of a rattle shook
from the emptying house.


    Love's bindings fell apart,
Love tumbled out and gasped and fled away
like a spirit escaped
    from the flesh; only the sighing of weeds
and the trembling mirrors
    of frost to mark its passing.


    Ah, Marta, the sorrow then!
The cloud-blotted moon, the sudden dark, the sound
of their hoof-iron clicking away
while the stones sleep on, and the forest sleeps,


    and we: the dreaded awakening...

# Journey on Water: A Prelude

When the noise of their paddles had ceased
and the craft was quiet,
borne unaided along the weedy shoreline
    by the slow-moving stream,
only the certain counting of water-beads dropping
    singly from the blades
of their extended paddles (it was as still as that):

We sat motionless there in the middle,
daring to breathe
    but not to meet each other's eyes –
just the feathers of your fingertips
resting on my hand, that told me many things.
    And they were also still,
their cloth-bound heads poised, listening
beyond the prow,
their broad, nude backs frozen against
    the gauze of light
that seemed half moonlight, half misted sunrise
– those hushed, expectant figures
molded with shadow, that just a while ago
had rippled like the river water.

    My thoughts were far away,
perhaps with the forest we had left behind
and through which, hour by hour,
we had lately drifted, borne on the dark stream,
    guided and sent along
by the deep, slow rhythm of their arms.
    It was quiet there,
the quiet that belongs to a sleeping forest, ever-
watchful, prophetic of waking:
    great trees looming inscrutable, dense,

from the river limits,
hung with vines and hairy mosses, spreading above
from either side, to meet and
sponge the milky light from the hidden sky.
     There was neither sound
or movement there above nor from the shores;
there was, no, not even a shiver
     of a leaf, the snap of a trodden twig;
hardly the slip and brush
of the water, or the steady plow of paddles
     lifting and dipping.
And I remember the chips of light that floated
across their backs and over
your silent face when the foliage above
     was sometimes thinned.

And the forest melted away
     as if some hand had rinsed the shoreline,
leaving a wash of luminous gray
that ran down the limits of sight and was lost
     in a sea of silent grass.
The marshlands stretched away into that light,
they seemed eternal.
     The spears and blades were soaked with dew,
and some would glisten faintly
as we drifted past, their stems swaying
     in the easy current.
And then the brown men quietly ceased their rhythm
and sat like hammered idols,
holding their dripping paddles, watching, listening
     somewhere ahead.

And now we felt the touch of dawn,
a warning shiver in the air;
     the light flickered and slowly expanded,
the landing was close at hand.

*59*

They moved and dipped their paddles again,
        sending us swiftly ahead.
Somewhere on the river margin a marshbird screamed
        and woke the world –
we halfway turned toward each other, saw
the pale, distracted features
faintly smiling in the clear, untroubled light.

# Landscapes

I

There is a land known to but a little sun,
the night has a way with it,
and the cold. There are rivers
there, not of water

and voices other than of life. Torrents hang
suspended as in a spell and
glitter with the starlight of their
eternal falling

through an endless space. And crude, unnatural
squeaks and mutterings
penetrate a thin and lifeless air, and
carry to the listening

mind a sense of ancient rockbeds slowly
scraped and carved by fields
of immeasurably moving ice; and that
which strains

the hearing is less of sound than of
inanimate life disturbed.
The night lets down its pale auroras,
an anesthetic dance

that sways across the static sleeper earth;
or moonlight filters down
and shows the massive dead its face,
a mirror wherein

eternity is reflected and known beyond all
revocation. But here this light
will cast no shadow to measure distance
by, nor will the fragile

air hold any but a dream of sound to guide
the visiting ear for long.
Upon a snowy rock I saw a frozen bird
singing a silent song.


II


Dark, wooded hills, the gloom of a stormy
twilight, a graveled road
that snakes along the crests and drops
between the rises;

the roadside bordered with sallow, matted grass
and thorny brush, the trees are
single on the sloping fields beyond,
stunted, rag-leaved,

bent away from some perpetual wind. The sooty clots
of low clouds bowl before that wind;
they drag no shadows across the road or fields,
there is not light

enough behind them – only the dull reddish foil
of the evening sky that smolders
beyond and floats its cast upon this ground.
The wind rushes out

of the gathering darkness, sending swirls of dead
leaves, sticks, and dust along the

road, crying and whimpering in the grass.
And now they come,

the halting stragglers of some brave excursion
winnowed by time. Scattered,
they seek, each for himself, a sign,
a known direction –

forgotten travelers. Some are on the road,
blinded with dust, garments
whipped in the wind, torn by thorns.
Some seek the fields,

stumbling through the tangled grass; they cry
out – their voices are lost
on the wind. Some huddle beneath
the trees and

do not move. And some come on, dragging,
limping, clutching their rags
about them; a few are together and
cling for anchor

against the blast. Their faces are thin and worn,
their eyes are red and swollen,
they cannot see ahead, dare not look
back lest hope fail

them. Now the sting of rain; they have come
to the end of light. The road
dips down beneath the storm, and then
there is the night.

IV. *California, 1952–54*

# Evening Change

Beautiful light down there
where the dark hills open
    toward the sea,
and the promontory groves
show like the ruined towers
of castles older than thought –
    Even this sordid valley
seems sweet and hallowed now,
where birds cross in the twilight,
unwatched by jealous eyes.

## Tomorrow

I see a city spreading on the plain,
its towers gleaming in the morning sun.

The clear air shows the highways
spoking out through tended fields
and on; and then beyond, the haze

of distant hills. I see the peace
that rises there to meet the day,

and wonder at the warmth, thinking
of that cold, forgotten night where
generations lie. But thinking's done,

and someone rises now from uneventful
slumber, to stand before an open

window, breathing on the waking town:
a lovely girl, who sees the world
as newly made – without its past,

dreamless of its future – who neither
sighs for love, nor knows I lived.

## Pawnee Dust

Goodbye, I see the horsemen mounting,
the lean dogs yapping in the dust.
Cottonwood pole and buffalo hide
are rolled and lashed, Gray Eagle's
woman carries the smoldering fire.

The young are laughing, they have no
burden yet, the broken camp is play.

Goodbye, the sun already rises,
bones of the last hunt whiten
in its rays. The plains are there
before you, beyond are grass
and water, vast untroubled herds.

Great Tirawa watches you, there's
nothing more to say. Good hunting west.

# Five Winter Stanzas

"Good hunting!" we cried,
and he turned to wave his hand
as he disappeared in the forest.

"Good hunting!" we cried again;
but it's likely he never heard us
behind the brow of the hill.

"Good hunting!" – that was the third,
and the sound of it hung in the air
above the snow and frost.

"Good hunting!" was barely an echo
as the days drew on
and the hunter hadn't returned.

"Good hunting!" died in our hearts
when April dripped from the eaves
and we knew he would never come.

# Ghost Town

Sun gone from the evening sky,
shadows reach on the plain,
the low hills turn from brown
to purple and slowly fade;
call of sleepy quail from the sage,
the road winds west,
a man rides into the dusk.

The streets of an empty town —
they lie in a dust that only
the wind disturbs. The sun
has hammered there and the rain
driven in. Buildings lean
together, gray, loose-boarded,
creaking when the wind blows.

Turn back to see it as it was.
Horses line the street, nosing
the rails. Wagons clatter by.
Dark men in dusty clothing,
pale men dressed for business,
outnumbered women. Shouts,
coarse laughter, music from a bar.

Behind those doors men sought
their pleasure, lay with it,
gambled for it, drank it down like
water, wept and cursed when
it was gone. Murder and justice
stained the floors and soaked
into the streets; the cries of

dead men lingered at high noon.
The streets led out to hill
and plain, men came and went and
did not leave their names.
Smell of dust and sweat and dung.
The sound of booted feet on the
boards, shod hoofs and wheels.

The road winds west, the rider
fades into the dusk. Moonrise
in the east, yelp of coyote from
the sage. Darkness on the plain,
shadows and silence in the town.
The wind rises from another
morning, where the rider goes.

# Verse

But time and change are misconstrued
if we refuse the oncoming of alteration
and, like the bear, seek some hidden
cave in which to perpetuate our
summer's fat and warmth, sleeping in
obese ignorance of the shaping winter.

We are not such hairy dreamers but that
it would be better for us to shrink
our flanks and stretch our sinews in
certain instinct to face the snaps
and hungers of a meager season; like

the close-boned, hunting wolf given to his
timeless part on nature's grimmest
stage; or like the snowy owl
drifting in savage patience over a land
from which all other birds, shaking
with the cold, have long since fled.

# Two Horses, One by the Roadside

A black horse standing
in an autumn field,
as still as though of stone;
behind him, pale
in the morning light,
the river mist.

Reminds me of a picture
I saw once of a stone horse
standing alone on
the plains of China,
part once of the
gateway to a palace.

Wind, frost, and many wars
had chipped their souvenirs;
the features marred,
there still remained the
essential form,
rooted, as though of the earth.

It gathered that lonely
country about it, a mark
to measure the silence of time.
And I remember a smile
was carved in its face,
the smile of a secret – the dreams
of emperors, perhaps.

And now this black horse,
living, bathed in the cold
light of another morning.

I passed and kept on
driving, the image
stored in my mind against
the day when that field
would be white with frost
and the horse led away
to a winter stall.

# Procession

Long, wavering files of ghostly children
clad in long, white gowns,
passing through the ancient, echoing manor.

Each carries a lighted candle, and the yellow
flame flickers on each innocent face.

No head is bowed, each looks before him
as room after room is passed,
each heavy door swung slowly open

at their approach: rooms silent
and bare of all save some faded tapestries

hung on the granite walls, and here and there
a suit of standing armor dully
gleaming as the flutter of their candles

throws sudden light into the corners,
lends the vaults a frieze of shadows

and, passing, leaves the rooms in former
darkness. The shuffle of their
footsteps down the stone corridors wakens

ancestral whispers; invisible guardians
watch them, the toil of centuries

precedes them in the smells and stains that
linger. Now the hours dwindle,
a grayness leaks from high slit windows

and shows the files before the last door,
halted there, their candles blowing out

in a freshening draft. And now begins
their gothic singing,
a sacred canon swelling on the heavy silence:

voice after voice beginning, summoning
echoes from countless forgotten

passages, ringing in the stones of buried
tombs. The great door slowly
swings, and overhead a bell begins to toll.

## Last Words on the Poet

He owed his enemies a debt of gratitude.
Enemy or friend, those who could not see,
excused from failure by their nature;
those who saw a little way, by laziness
or habit unable to see farther;
and those who followed nearly to the end,
then in some latent disposition
turned aside before their eyes knew light.

Acquaintance or relation, loved or not,
in ignorance and fear they set up walls
before him, switched the roadway signs
and sought to mine the very ground
beneath his feet. Some beckoned
from a pleasant meadow, bidding him
stay awhile; and others merely laughed
to see him climb the barriers,
stumbling at the crossways, and hesitate
before the smile and langour of reclining
ladies. But he could not condemn them,
their fortunes and solace were not his,
and likely enough their hearts
would have rejoiced if they had understood.

They had all served; their walls and
misdirections, snickerings and enticements,
only served to set his foot the firmer
and slowly teach his eyes to fasten
on the troubled slope ahead,
as tooth and claw develop keenness
in a hungry winter season.

Though blind before it all, his enemies
were spurs, through that perhaps
his friends; and those who turned away
disclosed the road he was to travel.

# Lineage

The sun of many autumns flames in my blood.

Here upon a hillside in the October wind
I know the end of every summer, and the feel
of that approaching silence is to me

a story told a million times.
I am not weary of that story, though I hear

the songs and praises of poets who died
with those regretted summers and left
the promised springs to other singers, turning

with a veiled salute into the coming cold.

The earth they knew remains. Despite the
swollen lives of men, I see the grass before
me and believe the dead could stand in

recognition here, braving another season.
Their words shape mine, their hearts expand again

in this remembered sun. And I am still,
and face the changeless autumn with a smile,
knowing that resurrection.

Poet, essayist, and teacher John Haines is the author of numerous collections of poems and critical essays, among which the most recent are *Fables and Distances: New & Selected Essays* (1996), *A Poems* (1993), and a memoir, *The Stars, The Snow, The Fire* (1989).

In 1995 Mr. Haines received a Literary Award from the American Academy of Arts & Letters. He has also been the recipient of a Lifetime Achievement Award from the Library of Congress, a Lenore Marshall / *The Nation* Award and fellowships from the Guggenheim Foundation and the National Endowment for the Arts. He has taught in recent years at Ohio University, George Washington University, and the University of Cincinnati. In 1993 he occupied the Chair in Creative Writing at Austin Peay State University in Tennessee.

Mr. Haines was born in 1924, and lives at this time in Anchorage, Alaska.

BOOK DESIGN & composition by John D. Berry Design, using Adobe PageMaker 6.0, a Power 120, and a Macintosh IIvx. The type is Sabon, designed in 1966 by Jan Tschichold. Sabon is based on the 16th-century types of Claude Garamond, and was designed as a functional and elegant text type that could be used simultaneously in hot metal on Monotype and Linotype typesetting machines and for hand-setting in metal foundry type. This is Linotype's digitized version of the typeface. *Printed by Malloy Lithographing.*